My City

by Lucy Long
illustrated by Holli Conger

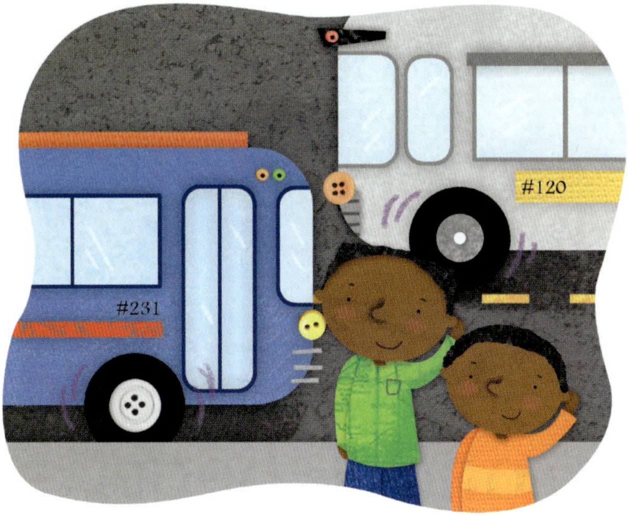

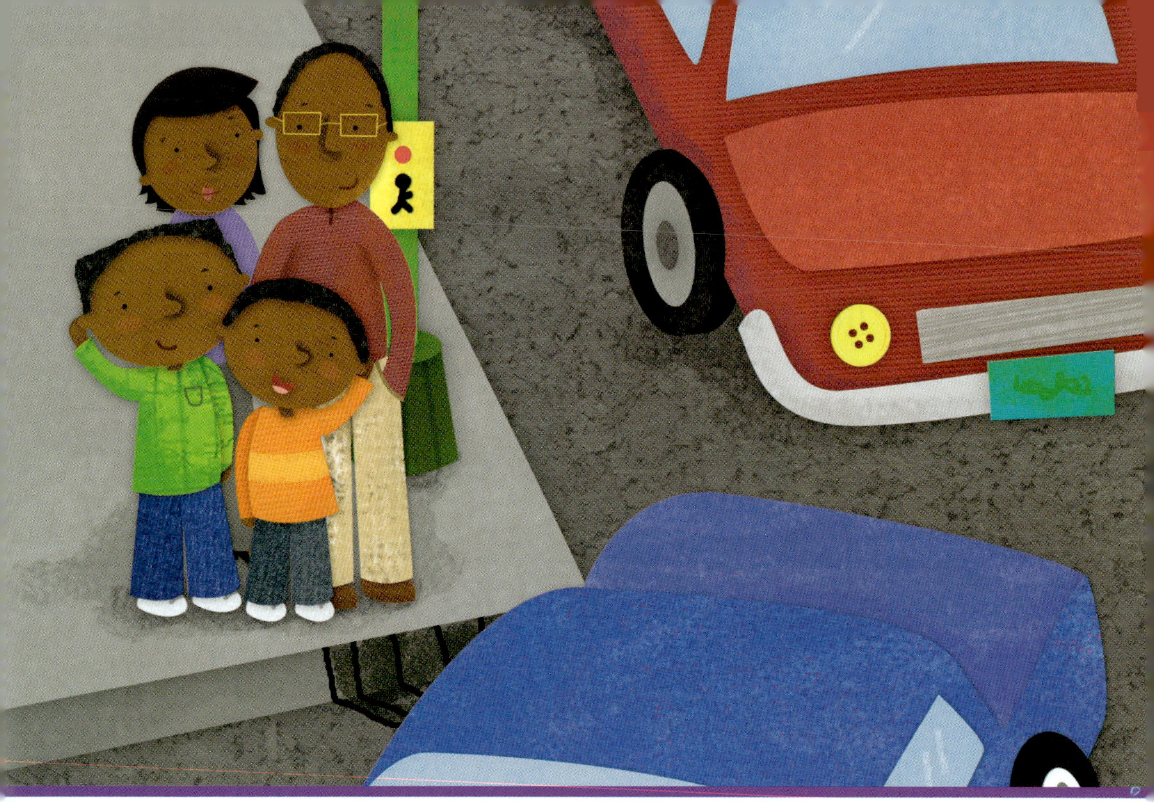

Ron and I hear 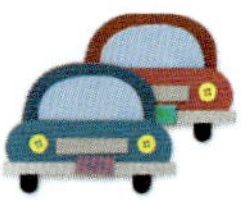 cars .

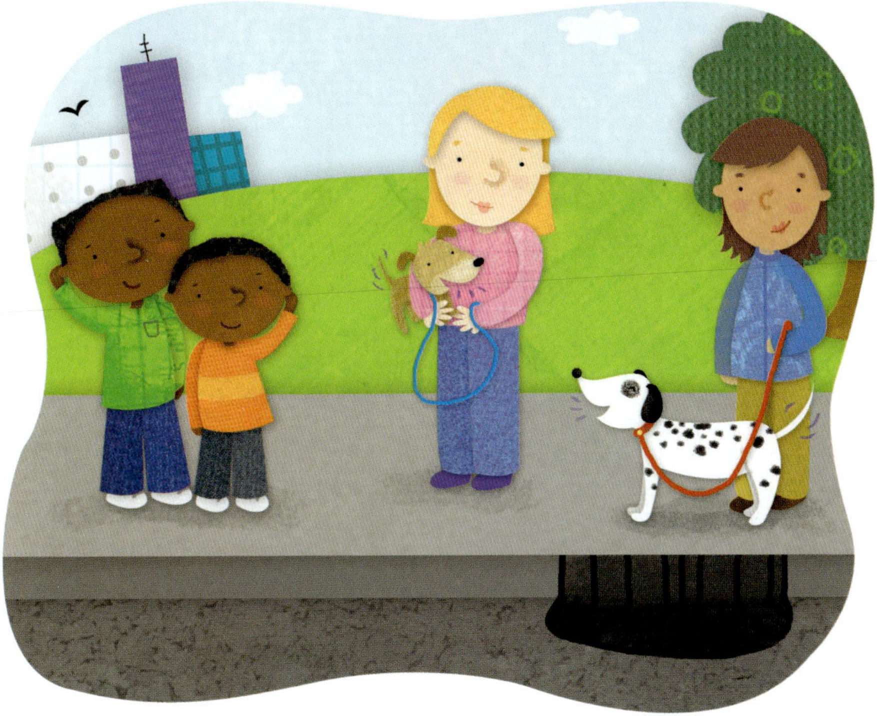

Ron and I hear 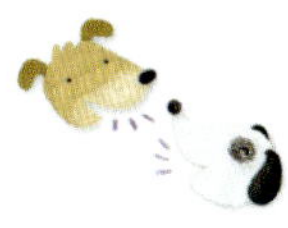 dogs .

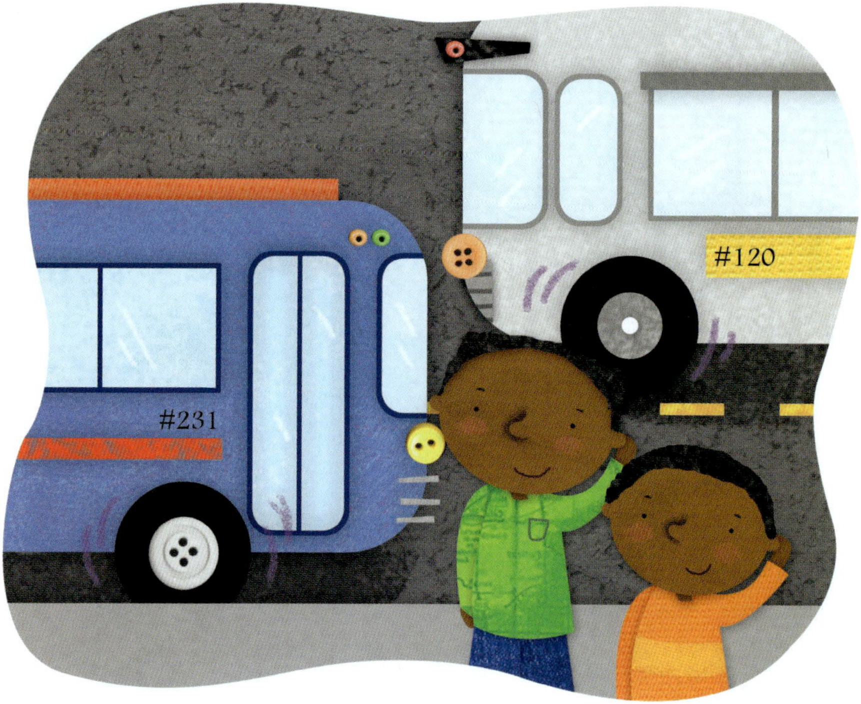

Ron and I hear 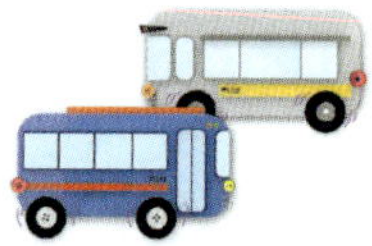 buses .

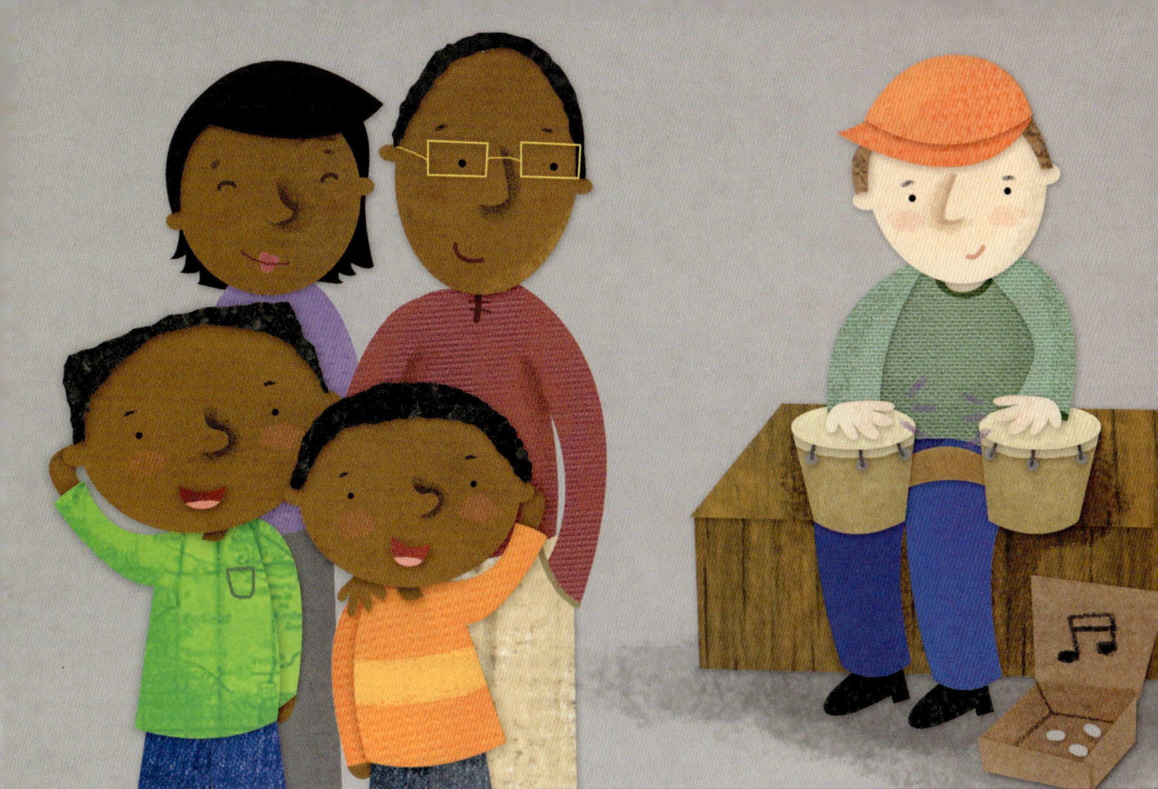

Ron and I hear 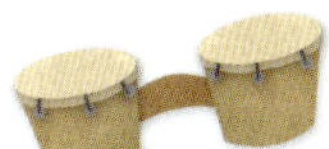 drums .

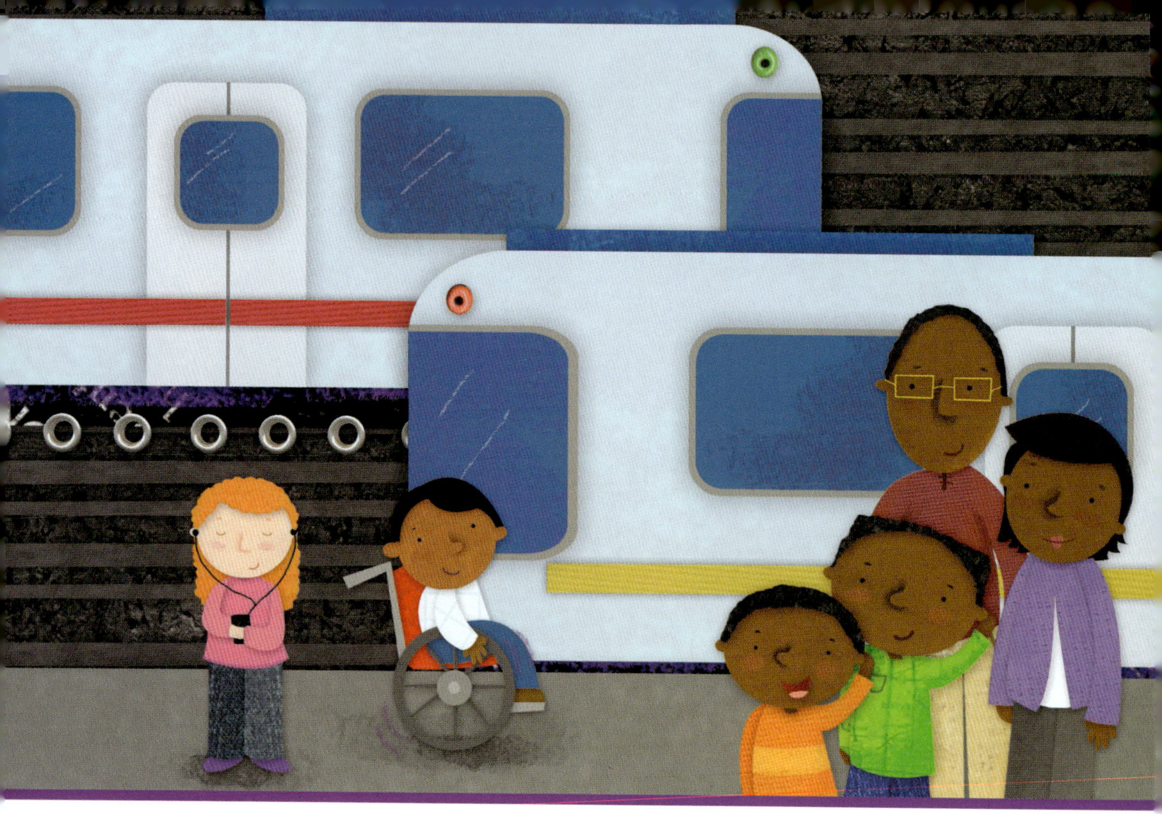

Ron and I hear 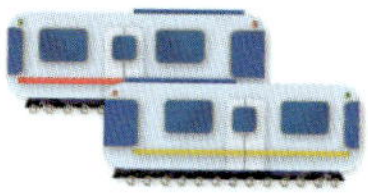 trains .

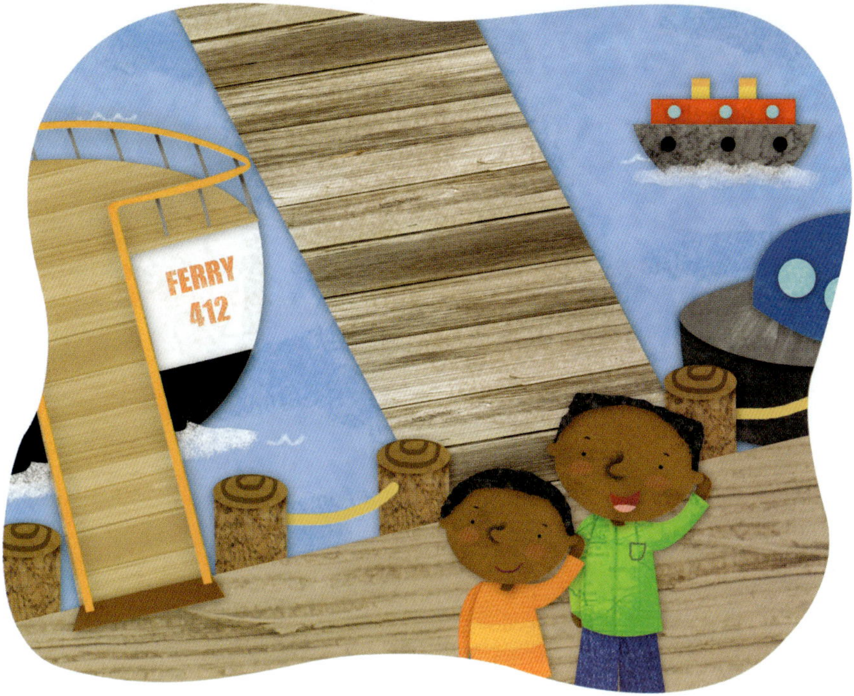

Ron and I hear 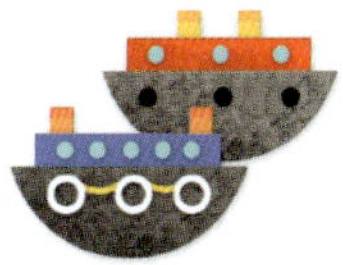 boats .

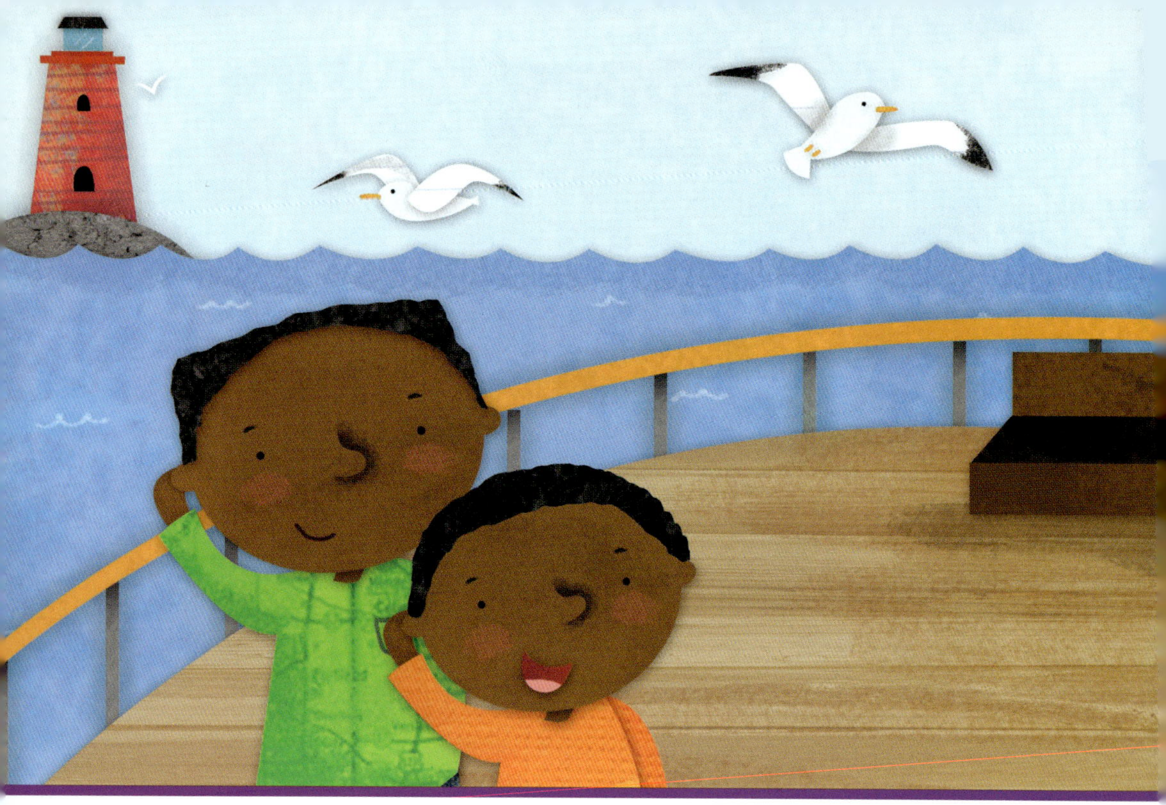

Ron and I have fun.